Hear the Just Word & Live It

Walter J. Burghardt, S.J.
Woodstock Theological Center

Paulist Press
New York/Mahwah, New Jersey

Cover/book design and interior illustrations by Nicholas T. Markell.

Library of Congress Cataloging-in-Publication Data

Burghardt, Walter J.
    Hear the just word & live it / Walter J. Burghardt.
        p.   cm. – (IlluminationBooks)
    Includes bibliographical references.
    ISBN 0-8091-3930-8 (alk. paper)
    1. Listening—Religious aspects—Catholic Church. 2. Communication—Religious aspects—Catholic Church. 3. Christianity and justice—Catholic Church. 4. Catholic preaching. I. Title: Hear the just word and live it. II. Title. III. Series.

BV4647.L56B87   2000
261.8—dc21

                                                    00-020170

Published by Paulist Press
997 Macarthur Boulevard
Mahwah, New Jersey 07430

www.paulistpress.com

Printed and bound in the
United States of America

Contents

IlluminationBooks

A Foreword

W hen this series was launched in 1994, I wrote that Illumination-Books were conceived to "bring to light wonderful ideas, helpful information, and sound spirituality in concise, illustrative, readable, and eminently practical works on topics of current concern."

In keeping with this premise, among the first books were offerings by well-known authors Joyce Rupp *(Little Pieces of Light...Darkness and Personal Growth)* and Basil Pennington *(Lessons from the Monastery That Touch Your Life)*. In addition, there were titles by up-and-coming authors and experts in the fields of spirituality and psychology. These books covered a wide array of topics: joy, controlling stress and anxiety, personal growth, discernment, caring for others, the mystery of the Trinity, celebrating the woman you are, and facing your own desert experiences.

The continued goal of the series is to provide great ideas, helpful steps, and needed inspiration in small volumes. Each of the books offers a new opportunity for the reader to explore possibilities and embrace practicalities that can be employed in everyday life. Thus, among the new and noteworthy themes for readers to discover are these: how to be more receptive to the love in our lives, simple ways to structure a personal day of recollection, a creative approach to enjoy reading sacred scriptures, and spiritual and psychological methods of facing discouragement.

Like the IlluminationBooks before them, forthcoming volumes are meant to be a source of support—without requiring an inordinate amount of time or prior preparation. To this end, each small work stands on its own. The hope is that the information provided not only will be nourishing in itself but also will encourage further exploration in the area.

When we view the world through spiritual eyes, we appreciate that sound knowledge is really useful only when it can set the stage for *metanoia*, the conversion of our hearts. Each of the IlluminationBooks is designed to contribute in some small but significant way to this process. So, it is with a sense of hope and warm wishes that I offer this particular title and the rest of the series to you.

–*Robert J. Wicks*
General Editor, IlluminationBooks

Introduction

*J*esus said, "Is a lamp brought in to be put under the bushel basket, or under the bed, and not on the lampstand? For there is nothing hidden, except to be disclosed, nor is anything secret, except to come to light. Let anyone with ears to hear listen!" *(Mk 4:21–23).*

More than three decades ago an insightful commentator, C. F. D. Moule, while recognizing how difficult it is to recapture the original setting and therefore the original meaning of the sayings in this section of Mark's Gospel, observed succinctly:

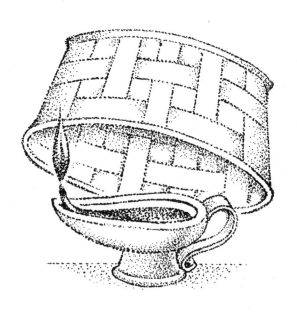

Hearing is meant to lead to discover
without discovering is like lighting a
then putting a cooking basin over it so that it goes
out again! Further, to hear without responding
with will and obedience is to lose what you hear—
to gain nothing from it. Only the man who is
ready himself to give—to give effort and willingness—will retain what he is given by others.[1]

Quite some time ago, after years of experience in
teaching, lecturing, and preaching, I came to a sobering
conclusion: Listening is not easy. In fact, listening is an
arduous art. You see, most conversations are not conversations at all. Either they are monologues: I wait patiently (or
impatiently) until you have finished—since civility
demands it—and then I say exactly what I would have said
if you had not spoken. Or they are debates: I do indeed listen, but only for that inept word or false phrase at which I
proceed to intercept and destroy. No, to listen is to give
myself totally, for that moment or hour, to another, to put
myself into the other's mind, yes the other's heart. It means
that I never hear naked words, always a human person.

Some of the most remarkable people in history
have been exceptional listeners. Call to mind the mother
of Jesus. In the context of Bethlehem, of angels announc-
ing "good news of great joy" and shepherds noising abroad
"what had been told them about this child," Luke tells us
that "Mary preserved all these things and pondered them
[literally, tossed them together] in her heart" (Lk 2:10, 17,
19). Recall Helen Keller, blind, mute, deaf, "listening" to
Annie Sullivan as if her life depended on it (it did indeed).

3

Think of St. John Vianney, the famous parish priest of Ars in France. Twelve hours a day in the confessional, he listened—not simply to sins somewhere out there, but to fractured hearts. And I shall never forget a singular scholar of early Christianity at the Catholic University of America, Johannes Quasten. Several times he said to us doctoral candidates with quiet sincerity, "I learn as much from my students as my students learn from me." He actually listened to us...and discovered...and responded.

Closer to our own time, I am deeply indebted to Benedictine Rembert Weakland, archbishop of Milwaukee, for his willingness to listen to voices in strong disagreement with him, voices advocating freedom to choose abortion, ready to listen even at the expense of Vatican displeasure. Take one of his reflections on that level:

> I need to listen, though nothing may come of it. I often think I know exactly what needs to be done, but I'm terribly wrong sometimes. I need to speak both to those who are my friends and to those who are not my friends. But in real dialogue. If you want to exercise any meaningful authority in the Church today, you have to listen not just to the most agreeable voices, and not solely to the edicts of Rome. Rather, you listen to where the Spirit is—you hear one small voice, and you say, "That's it!" Not consensus—that's no way to lead. I'm surely influenced by the third chapter of the Rule of St. Benedict. When anything important is brewing, you call the community together and listen for the Spirit. And

you allow the youngest, least experie/
to speak first, so he won't be overw
the experts.[2]

The problem is, to listen is to risk. It takes your precious time, often when you can least afford it. You take on other people's problems, when you have enough of your own. It means getting involved. For if you listen, you open yourself: parents to their children, CEOs to subordinates, bishops to the laity, even (God save the mark!) teachers to students. If you're a good listener, people "dump" on you. If you listen, someone may fall in love with you—and that can be a burden you may not care to bear.

A different kind of risk startles us in the King Herod who imprisoned John the Baptist. Mark tells us, "Herod feared John, knowing that he was a just and holy man, and he protected him. When he heard him, he was greatly perplexed [or: he used to raise many questions], and *he liked to listen to him*" (Mk 6:20). The problem arose when he listened to his dancing daughter Herodias. It meant a choice: on the one hand, his pleasure in the wisdom of a good man; on the other, an ill-advised oath and his fear of being embarrassed in front of his guests. When the moment of truth arrived, he heard not John but Herodias requesting John's head. "The king was deeply grieved; but..." (v. 26).

Still, the risk can be matched by a matchless joy. For listening, really listening, is an act of love; and so it is wonderfully human, splendidly Christian. More human, more Christian, than sheer knowledge. I used to think, in

.ny youthful arrogance, that what I had to offer the Catholic world, even the more generally Christian world, was a hatful of answers. I do have some, rarely original. More importantly, I come to others as I am, with my own ignorance, my own weakness, my own sinfulness, my own fears and tears. I share not so much words as myself; I am there. Not primarily my ear or my tongue; simply I.

It's allied to what two treasured friends of mine, long-term activists Msgr. George Higgins in Washington, D.C., and Msgr. John Egan in Chicago, have found gratifyingly effective: the ministry or sacrament of presence. Such, I submit, is basic to our Christian mission: to be where another can reach out to us.

Another reason why listening is all-important? I remember my teacher and colleague John Courtney Murray declaring, "I do not know what I have said until I understand what you have heard." Communication is not a one-way street. Whether it's public proclamation or colloquial conversation, what you heard is not necessarily what I tried to say. The fault may lie on either side, on my lack of clarity or your failure to genuinely listen.

Worth hearing here is Presbyterian preacher and novelist Frederick Buechner, as he expresses his own experience in his short autobiography:

> We are so used to hearing what we want to hear and remaining deaf to what it would be well for us to hear that it is hard for us to break the habit. But if we keep our hearts and minds open as well as our ears, if we listen with patience and hope, if we

remember at all deeply and honestly, then I think we come to recognize, beyond all doubt, that, however faintly we may hear [God], he is indeed speaking to us, and that, however little we may understand of it, his word to each of us is both recoverable and precious beyond telling.[3]

But enough of generalizations, however true. In down-to-earth, detailed, concrete reality, what does listening, hearing, involve? Not to bog down in abstractions, I shall focus on an issue agonizingly real, ever so current, unparalleled in the number of areas, life situations, it covers. I mean...justice. My approach will move out from a project I conceived and codirect, Preaching the Just Word. As the title indicates and you will soon see, our emphasis in the project is on more effective preaching or proclamation, more effective communication. But the proclamation is not self-sufficient. If the proclamation is to be effective, if communication is to take place, someone must be listening; preaching the just word must be complemented by hearing the just word. Though aware of this, I have never quite concentrated on it to the extent I have on the proclamation. The major thrust of this book has precisely the listener, the listening, in mind. But this demands an extended preliminary word on *what* it is we ought to be hearing. What is this just word that confronts the Christian disciple?

Chapter One

The Just Word: What Is It?

*F*irst then, the prerequisite to listening: someone speaking, a word spoken. My project Preaching the Just Word is a first stage in a process. It is an effort to improve the quality of justice preaching across our country.[4] This involves, to begin with, a content. What is the justice to which we extend a priority in this project? In 1987 a gently passionate Jesuit social scientist, the late Philip Land, opened an encyclopedia article on justice with a quotation from the Hebrew prophet Amos, whose career in Israel took place during a period of social and religious corruption:

"Let justice roll down like waters" (Amos 5:24). Land continued:

> Prior to Vatican II no Roman Catholic treatise on justice would have begun with scripture. It would have taken its start from the [ethical] definition of justice...to render to each [what is] one's due and proceeded then to analyze in the light of reason the various relations this involves. With Vatican II but especially with the 1971 Synod, Justice in the World, justice becomes a call to the Christian from the God of the two Testaments.[5]

That call is not primarily to ethical justice, not primarily a demand to give each man, woman, and child what they deserve, what they can claim as a strict right, because it can be proven from philosophy, from sheer reason. Nor is the call primarily to legal justice, whose symbol, a blindfolded lady with scales and a sword, promises impartiality. I am not downplaying ethical and legal justice. Without them life would degenerate into a jungle, the survival of the fittest, the preserve of the strong, the shrewd, and the savage. Even so, God's call is to a justice richer still, breath-taking in its breadth and depth. We term it biblical justice.

Biblical justice

What, then, is biblical justice? More than two decades ago, Scripture scholar John R. Donahue shaped a working definition with admirable succinctness:

In general terms the biblical idea of justice can be described as *fidelity to the demands of a relationship.* In contrast to modern individualism the Israelite is in a world where "to live" is to be united with others in a social context either by bonds of family or by covenant relationships. This web of relationships—king with people, judge with complainants, family with tribe and kinfolk, the community with the resident alien and suffering in their midst and all with the covenant God—constitutes the world in which life is played out.[6]

The critical point here, not only for Israel but for every human person? Life is relationships—on earth as in heaven, for us and for the Trinity.

Within this context, in what sense is God just? Because God always acts as God should, is invariably faithful to God's promises, e.g. defending or vindicating God's people, punishing violations of the covenant, never forgetting a forgetful people. It is stunningly exemplified when the people complain, "The LORD has forsaken me, my lord has forgotten me," and the LORD replies:"Can a woman forget her nursing child, or show no compassion for the child of her womb? Even these may forget, yet I will not forget you. See, I have inscribed you on the palms of my hands" (Isa 49:14–16a). Time and again the Psalms proclaim God's fidelity, God's faithfulness. "All [the LORD's] work is done in faithfulness" (Ps 33:4). "Your steadfast love is as high as the heavens; your faithfulness extends to the clouds" (Ps 57:10). "You, O LORD, are slow to anger and abounding in steadfast love and faithfulness" (Ps 86:15). "The faithfulness of the LORD endures for ever" (Ps 117:2). "Your faithfulness endures to all generations" (Ps 119:90).

Nor may we forget God's only Son, sped to the wilderness by the Spirit, to be tested by Satan (Mt 4:1–11). "The testing," a fine New Testament scholar notes, "will show forth the *fidelity* of the Son of God."[7]

When are people just? When they are in right relationship in each area of their lives: to their God, to their sisters and brothers, and to the whole of created reality. The Israelites were to love the Lord their God with all their mind and heart, all their soul and strength; they were to reject all idols that, like the golden calf, threatened to replace the one true God. They were to father the fatherless and mother the motherless, welcome the stranger, feed the sojourner, show hospitality to the resident alien, not because the orphan and the outsider deserved it, but because this was the way God had acted with Israel. A text in Deuteronomy is telling: "Love the sojourner [the stranger, the resident alien], for you were sojourners in the land of Egypt" (Deut 10:19). In freeing the oppressed, they were mirroring the loving God who had delivered *them* from oppression, had freed them from Pharaoh.

In the Book of Exodus God details this kind of justice with solemn commands:

> You shall not wrong or oppress a resident alien, for you were aliens in the land of Egypt. You shall not abuse any widow or orphan. If you do abuse them, when they cry out to me I will surely heed

their cry....If you lend money to my people, to the poor among you, you shall not deal with them as a creditor; you shall not exact interest from them. If you take your neighbor's cloak in pawn, you shall restore it before the sun goes down; for it may be your neighbor's only clothing to use as cover; in what else shall that person sleep? And if your neighbor cries out to me, I will listen, for I am compassionate. (Exod 22:21–27)

Right relationship not only to God and the people of God but to the things of God as well. Crucial here is God's command to the first humans, "Have dominion" (Gen 1:28). Despite all the accusations leveled (at times justifiably) against Christians' recourse to the Genesis text, God's command does not justify exploiting nature for human convenience. The "dominion" is exercised by humans as God's images, reflecting the Creator who looked on all that divinity had shaped "and indeed it was very good" (Gen 1:31). The mandate given humanity in Eden is not exploitation but reverential care for God's creation. Humans stand to nature in a relationship of stewards or caretakers. A steward is one who manages what is someone else's. A steward cares, is concerned, agonizes. Stewards may not plunder or waste; they are responsible, can be called to account for their stewardship. As the Psalmist phrased it, "The earth is the LORD's, and all that is in it" (Ps 24:1).

Justice and Jesus

It is the Israelite idea of justice that sparked the ministry of Jesus. He summed it up, in a sense, in the synagogue at Nazareth: "The Spirit of the Lord is upon me, for [the Lord] has anointed me, has sent me to preach good news to the poor, to proclaim release for prisoners and sight for the blind, to send the downtrodden away relieved" (Lk 4:18). For Jesus, too, the just man or woman is not primarily someone who gives to another what that other deserves. Jesus inaugurates a new covenant, where the most significant relationship is the monosyllable that says it all: love—and astonishingly, where loving one's neighbor, already commanded in Leviticus (19:18), is said by Jesus to be "like" loving God (Mt 22:29). Not a psychological balancing act: As much or as little as you love yourself, that much love or that little love shower on your neighbor. No, "love one another as I have loved you" (Jn 15:12). This is what is unique in the new covenant cut by God in the blood of God's Son.

In brief, Jesus' whole ministry had for its purpose to make all relationships right: e.g., the adulterer and the tax collector set right with God; the man possessed and the ostracized leper restored to their families; the blind beggar Bartimaeus rejoined to the community; yes, scribes and Pharisees freed from their legalism and open anew to a God who prefers mercy to sacrifice.

In 1975, Pope Paul VI insisted that there are two realities inseparable from evangelization: Jesus Christ and people. Jesus Christ, because without Christ as the centerpiece, there is no genuine evangelization. People, because "evangelization cannot be complete unless account is taken of the links between the gospel and the concrete personal and social life of men and women....The Church considers it highly important to establish structures which are more

human, more just, more respectful of the rights of the person, less oppressive and coercive."[8]

In the crucifixion of Christ and his resurrection, the single, triadic community (God, humans, and nature) that flourished like a primitive Camelot in such intimate communion for so brief a space in Eden is once again possible—humans at peace with God, humans at peace with one another, humans and nonhuman creation at peace each with the other. Again possible because "if anyone is in Christ, there is a new creation" (2 Cor 5:17). Sin loses not all its power but surely its dominion—so much so that Jesus can pray to his Father, "I in them and you in me, that they may become perfectly one" (Jn 17:23). And not only creatures of intelligence and love. God's "plan for the fullness of time" was "to gather *all things* in [Christ], things in heaven and things on earth" (Eph 1:10). In John Paul II's startling declaration, Christians must "realize that their responsibility within creation and their duty toward nature and the Creator are *an essential part of their faith.*"[9]

Very simply, our imaginative God still has in mind a single community, in which the Creator and all creation live in a harmony that sin cannot substantially corrupt, an interdependence of man, woman, and nature that is an essential facet of salvation's story.

My point here is that in God's plan salvation takes place within a single, all-embracing community. My salvation depends on my fidelity to three relationships: Do I love God above all else? Do I love each sister and brother as Jesus has loved and loves me? Do I touch each "thing" with the reverence God asked of humankind at its birthing?

A final facet: Indispensable though it is, preaching or proclaiming the just word is only a stage, one aspect, in a process. A homily, for example, in fact the liturgy as a whole, does not attempt to *solve* complex social, political, or economic problems: welfare or workfare, racist housing contracts, public monies for private and parochial schools, bombs over Iraq or Serbia, voting for prochoice Catholic candidates, wages for child workers in Indonesia, land for the Palestinians, education and health benefits for the children of illegal immigrants, and many others. A homily should raise consciousness, lift awareness. Other modes of proclamation may delve more deeply into justice issues. But in either case, if the proclamation is to be effective, someone must be listening. But...to whom?

Chapter Two
Listen to Jesus

More than a generation ago, Dominican Fergus Kerr insisted that "Doing theology at all depends on hearing the word of God: God must be allowed to speak to us before we can begin to speak about him."[10] Much the same is true of our response to the just Word: God must be allowed to speak to us if we are to respond.

For a splendid beginning, give ear to Jesus. Such was the command of the Father from the cloud at the hill of transfiguration: "This is my Son, the Beloved; with him I am well pleased. Listen to him!" (Mt 17:5). A command not only to the favored three, Peter, James, and John; a command to all God's children. Why listen to him? Because he is *the* Word, the Word the Father speaks from all eternity, the Word in our flesh. Never has God spoken quite like this, so personally, in our own human language. "Of old," the New Testament Letter to the Hebrews opens, "God spoke to our ancestors in many and various ways, but in these last days He has spoken to us by a Son" (Heb 1:1-2). Not by angels; by the God-man. "Therefore we must pay greater attention to what we have heard, so that we do not drift away from it" (2:1).

Christ present in his word

But how does Jesus speak *to us?* After all, his sandals no longer scuff the dust of Palestine, his voice no longer shivers the Mideast air. The Second Vatican Council rings loud and clear: "[Christ] is present in his word, since it is he himself who speaks to us when the holy Scriptures are read in the church."[11] Do you believe that? Do you really believe what you say, "[This is] the word of the Lord"? Do you actually believe this is the Lord Jesus speaking to you? If you do, how do you listen to him? As breathlessly as Moses listened to the Lord God on Mount Sinai? As open to God's word as was the young Mary in Nazareth? Do you "marvel," like Jesus' townspeople, at the "gracious words," the "words of grace," that fall from his lips (Lk 4:22)? Or has repetition dulled your senses, so that Christ is less charismatic than Oprah?

The thrilling fact is, this Jesus who speaks to us in the word proclaimed is not a character out of a dead past. Listening to Scripture in the liturgy is not the same as reading Augustine's *Confessions* or Gibran's *Prophet,* not the same as hearing a Shakespeare sonnet or Handel's *Messiah*. When the Scriptures are read to you, Jesus himself speaks to you. Now. This is not pious pap for infants; this is Christian realism. This is not a recital by a reader chosen for powerful lungs and a clear voice. Here is the risen Christ, incomparably alive, addressing us, challenging us, encouraging us, admonishing us, no less than when he preached from Peter's boat, no less than when he thundered from a hilltop, "You have heard, but I say to you...." It calls for a response similar to the reaction of the two discouraged disciples greeted by an unrecognized Jesus on the way to Emmaus: "Were not our hearts burning within us while he was talking to us on the road, while he was opening the Scriptures to us?" (Lk 24:32).

The Scriptures. Not only the New Testament; not only the Gospels, the Pauline epistles, John's letters, Revelation. "Do not think," Jesus declared, "that I have come to abolish the law or the prophets; I have come not to abolish but to fulfill" (Mt 5:17). The expression "the law and the prophets" is a formula frequent in Matthew for the whole of God's revelation in the Prior Testament. That revelation would indeed be brought to completion through Christ, with Christ, in Christ; but it would not be abolished. It is the whole of God's revelation that Jesus proclaims. We do him and ourselves an injustice when we simply tolerate "the law and the prophets" till we come to *the* Gospel.

The readings at liturgy are dangerous words. Not only because it is God's Son, Jesus Christ, speaking to us; equally dangerous because of what he is saying. What happens, what is my reaction, when I hear Jesus announce his

ministry in the synagogue of his native Nazareth: "The Spirit of the Lord is upon me; for [the Lord] has anointed me; He has sent me to preach good news to the poor, to proclaim release for prisoners and sight for the blind, to send the downtrodden away relieved, and to proclaim the Lord's year of favor" (Lk 4:18–19)? Especially when Jesus sits down and declares to his fellow Jews, "Today this scripture has been fulfilled in your hearing" (v. 21). Today, right now, as you sit listening.

As I sit listening, is this sheer history to me? "Today," for Luke, is not restricted to the Period of Jesus alone; Luke sees fulfillment taking place as well in the Period of the Church.[12] Remember Dr. Moule above? Hearing leads to discovery; discovery should lead to a response. Sending the downtrodden away relieved is not the ministry of Jesus alone. It began indeed in Nazareth; it continues through his brothers and sisters in every age till his kingdom comes in its fullness. Nothing Jesus speaks to me in the liturgy—the readings, the homily, the prayers—is meant to disappear into thin air. The poor, the imprisoned in so many ways, the downtrodden; those who thirst like the Samaritan woman at the well, those who walk in deeper darkness than the man born blind, those who are dead in more ways than Lazarus— they surround us...today. They call out to us, mutely or angrily...today.

Not that we are all called to the same response. Back in the third and fourth centuries, well-to-do Antony of Egypt, in his late teens, walked into a church and listened. Listened to a Gospel, listened as our Lord counseled a rich young man, heard Jesus during the liturgy, "If you wish to be perfect, sell your possessions and give [the money] to the poor, and come, follow me" (Mt 19:21). He did. Through 85 years he was a hermit at heart, in desire; but the world beat a path to his door. The sick and the heartsore, the wealthy and the beggared, philosopher and soldier and monk, all stormed his solitude.[13]

Others Jesus addresses differently. An Ignatius Loyola he inspires to found a religious community that will work with the downtrodden, console the sick, educate young minds, travel across the world to unearth the Christ who is already there but not quite recognized. To a Peter Maurin he gives the courage to found *The Catholic Worker*, to live with society's rejects.

What is it I hear when Jesus says that on Judgment Day he will say to some, "Come, inherit the kingdom. For I was hungry and you gave me food, I was thirsty and you gave me something to drink, I was a stranger and you welcomed me, I was naked and you gave me clothing, I was sick and you took care of me, I was in prison and you visited me" (Mt 25:34-36)? Does it get through to me that my relationship to Christ, intimate or lukewarm, real or nonexistent, depends on my relationship to the disadvantaged, to the hungry on my street, to the immigrant denied healthcare, to the sick and lonely in my parish, to the million youngsters who sleep on America's streets each night, to the several thousand on Death Row across the country? Does it shiver me to realize that my eternal salvation may well depend on the men, women, and children I come across each day, the foreigner/victim whom I pass by "on the other side" like the priest in the story of the Good Samaritan (Lk 10:29–37)?

We are told that Dorothy Day could not feed on the body and blood of Jesus in Communion and be insensitive to the fact that someone was hungry; could not be warmed by the Eucharist while her brothers and sisters did not have a blanket to cover them; could not blithely "go to the altar of God" aware that someone was sleeping over a grate on a bitterly cold sidewalk.

What does Jesus say to *me*? If I hear nothing, where is the blockage?

A consistent ethic of life

"Choose life," Yahweh commanded the Israelites through Moses, and Jesus commands Catholic Christians in the liturgy (Deut 30:19). What do I hear? John Paul II has listened, discovered, responded. In January 1999, in St. Louis, after referring to the infamous Dred Scott decision that declared African Americans property, outside the national community and constitutional protection, he said: "Today, the conflict is between a culture that affirms, cherishes, and celebrates the gift of life, and a culture that seeks to declare entire groups of human beings—the unborn, the terminally ill, the handicapped, and others considered 'unuseful'—to be outside the boundaries of legal protection."[14]

Is my response a consistent ethic of life? Life in the womb and life near the tomb. A million and a half abortions each year in the United States, 50 million across the world—does this arouse my rage for an unrecognized endangered species, or has it become for me, as for all too many Christians, simply a fact of contemporary culture? Am I so mesmerized by Supreme Court decisions that I hear no other voices?

A respected *Washington Post* columnist, George F. Will, in an article titled "The Fruits of *Roe v. Wade*,"[15] noted that, in a 1992 abortion decision, "the court, declaring abortion a right central to 'autonomy,' gaseously said, 'At the heart of liberty is the right to define one's own concept of existence, of meaning, of the universe, and of the mystery of human life.'" Mr. Will listened to the Supreme Court, listened to the 9th Circuit Court's affirmation of a constitutional right to make "decisions that are highly personal and intimate, as well as of great importance to the individual," and responded:

> But, then, why not also declare constitutionally sacrosanct a decision—personal, intimate, important—to use heroin? Or to practice consensual incest or polygamy? Who is to gainsay a person's—or a judge's—contention that such practices accord with his definition of existence, or meaning, or the universe, or life's mystery?

"Choose life." Gaining notoriety and strength in our country is a Kevorkian crusade for physician-assistance suicide. The crusade is fueled by Dr. Kevorkian's personal participation in scores of suicides, and by his challenge to the courts to judge him, to imprison him. Indeed we have to listen, to the doctor and to those who seek his aid in dying, but not only to them.

"Choose life." Allow me extra space for a troublesome instance in a consistent ethic of life: What do I hear about capital punishment? Recent polls "show that support for capital punishment is as high as 75 percent among Catholics in the south and a sizeable majority of Catholics favour it in other parts of the nation."[16] The justice question: To whom am I listening? Whom do I hear?

Is it simply to the majority of Catholic voices? Important to hear their side, of course. But what of their arguments? Some seemingly boil down to vengeance, an eye for an eye. I recall a firm affirmation in both Old and New Testaments, "Vengeance is mine, says the Lord" (Deut 32:25; Rom 12:19).

Some argue, or assume, that capital punishment cuts down on crime. Have they listened to Manhattan District Attorney Robert Morgenthau? "Prosecutors must reveal the dirty little secret they too often share only among themselves: The death penalty actually hinders the fight against crime." Capital punishment "is a mirage that distracts society from more fruitful, less facile answers. It exacts a terrible price in dollars, lives and human decency. Rather than tamping down the flames of violence, it fuels them while draining millions of dollars from more promising efforts to restore safety to our lives."[17]

Some argue that an execution brings closure to the families of victims. Then let them listen to an emotional outburst from Larry Post, father of a murdered daughter, speaking for himself and his wife:

How dare the [Supreme Court] speak for me, my family and my murdered daughter [Lisa] when it says: "Only with finality can the victims move forward knowing the moral judgment will be carried out."...If they are referring to the victims' families, what about all those who are opposed to the death penalty, such as myself and family members belonging to the national organization Murder Victims Families for Reconciliation and those countless others, who remain silent but don't want any more killings? ...My daughter would not have wanted to see anyone killed, and especially not in her name.[18]

Have they listened to John Paul II? He has argued that "as a result of steady improvements in the organization of the penal system, such cases [i.e., where only through execution is defense of society possible] are very rare, if not practically nonexistent."[19] Even more strongly in St. Louis: "The dignity of human life must never be taken away, even in the case of someone who has done great evil."

Have they listened to the muted cries from the minorities on Death Row? Richard Dieter, director of the Death Penalty Information Center in Washington, D.C., points out that while African Americans comprise about 12 percent of the U.S. population, they account for 43 percent of prisoners on Death Row and 36 percent of those executed; of the 510 executed since the Supreme Court returned the question to the individual states in 1977, at least 34 of those executed were designated as retarded.

Adjoining my lodgings in Washington, D.C., is the McKenna Center, named after the late Horace McKenna, S.J., and continuing his extraordinary service to the poor, the homeless, the hungry. The cook at this Jesuit-run center is African-American Joseph Brown, known to his friends as Shabaka. Shabaka spent almost 15 years on Florida's Death Row. There, as in most other states that subscribe to capital punishment, a majority of his cellmates were from minorities, some were retarded, and almost all were poor. Shabaka was eventually found to be innocent. After 14 years behind bars. Listen to Shabaka as he reflects on his experience:

> Racism plays a big part in [the criminal justice system]. You can't expect a country like this with a long history of slavery to overturn it in a night's time. If you'd been at my trial in Florida, you'd have thought you were at a K.K.K. meeting and I was the guest of honor. I was the only black person in the whole courtroom. The jury was all white.[20]

On my last reading, 49 women were on Death Row in the United States. Most are kept in isolation 23 hours a day and are not allowed contact visitors. Robin Rowe, on Death Row in Idaho, has not seen another person in four years except the guards who bring her meals and accompany her to the exercise cage. Are the forms of execution clean? Does the condemned woman die with dignity? Not so, says Kathleen O'Shea, author of *Women and the Death Penalty in the United States, 1900–1998.* "In the 17 states that have women on death row, women may be hanged, shot by a firing squad, given cyanide gas to inhale, electrocuted or given a poison through an intravenous drip." Some executions have been botched, causing prolonged agonizing deaths. "There is no way to take a life with dignity, if it's not that person's time to go."[21]

No one denies that innocent people have been executed. The only argument is, how many? And now that a bill has passed Congress drastically shortening the time for filing a habeas corpus petition at the Federal level in order to introduce new evidence, Death Row inhabitants stand in even greater danger.

Ultimately, I submit, there is a single overriding question to which each of us must listen, one question each of us has to answer: How sacred is *every* human life? And whatever my answer, why do I answer as I do? Perhaps one has to hear Death Row counselor Sister Helen Prejean—or watch her film *Dead Man Walking.*

Incidental, yet not quite trivial: Under "listening" headings *The NRSV [New Revised Standard Version] Concordance Unabridged* (1991) has 393 entries for the whole of Scripture, "Including the Apocryphal/Deuterocanonical Books." From Genesis to Revelation, God, God's Son, and God's servants are constantly pleading with individuals and institutions to listen. Yahweh pleads with Cain, "Listen! Your brother's blood is crying out to me from the ground!" (Gen 4:10). Pleads with the people, "O Israel, if you would but listen to me!" (Ps 81:8). The preacher Ecclesiastes warns, "Guard your steps when you go to the house of God; to draw near to listen is better than the sacrifice offered by fools" (Eccl 5:1). Jesus says solemnly to the scribes and Pharisees, "The queen of the South will rise up at the judgment with this generation and condemn it, because she came from the ends of the earth to listen to the wisdom of Solomon, and see, something greater than Solomon is here!" (Mt 12:42). In the very last book the Son of Man says time and again, "Let anyone who has an ear listen to what the Spirit is saying to the churches" (Rev 2:7, 11, 17, 29; 3:6, 13, 22).

Chapter Three

Listen to the Church

"A ha!" you say. "Here it comes, the last just word. Forget the reasoning, the argument, the dialogue, the individual conscience. 'The Church says....'" Sorry to disappoint you. The Church is not the pope, not the Congregation for the Doctrine of the Faith, not the college of bishops, no, not even the pastor! The Church is, as the very early believers insisted, "the 'We' of Christians." The Catholic Church is a community of believers, a people. And this touches intimately our effort to hear the whole of the just word.

I am persuaded that what the Second Vatican Council said of divine revelation can be transferred to the entire effort to reach truth, including the search for the just word.

> [The] tradition which comes from the apostles develops in the Church with the help of the Holy Spirit. For there is a growth in the understanding of the realities and the words which have been handed down. This happens through the contemplation and study made by believers, who treasure these things in their hearts (cf. Lk 2:19, 51), through the intimate understanding of spiritual things they experience, and through the preaching of those who have received through episcopal succession the sure gift of truth. For, as the centuries succeed one another, the Church constantly moves forward toward the fullness of divine truth until the words of God reach their complete fulfillment in her.[22]

Listening to the whole Church

Listening to the Church on justice issues means listening to the *whole* Church: to official statements from popes and bishops, and to the ceaseless struggles of lay-folk, priests, and deacons to grasp and express what "fidelity to the demands of our relationships"—to God, to people, and to the earth—exacts of us within the signs of our times. A word on each.

Official statements? Not ordinary reading matter for Catholics in the United States. For several reasons. Some documents are discouragingly long; an outdated rhetoric often speaks to the head far more than to the heart;

cafeteria Catholics have already decided what to accept and what to reject. I suggest that on social issues the hierarchy is often in the forefront of serious discussion and offers challenges to which few Catholics can afford to turn a deaf ear.

Take the synod of bishops that convened in Rome in 1971: 190 bishops, 14 Oriental patriarchs, 19 curial prefects, 15 papal appointees, and ten superiors general of male orders. Obvious, even at this distance, was minimal lay involvement; Lady Jackson (Barbara Ward) was an outstanding exception. On the credit side, half the bishops were from the Third World; the Latin American bishops came with the mind-shaking experience of their 1968 meeting at Medellín, Colombia.

One of the synod's documents was titled *Justice in the World*.[23] So much therein demands hearing today.[24] First, in a significant breakthrough the synod insisted that "action on behalf of justice fully appears to us a constitutive dimension of the preaching of the gospel." You may argue, as some have, whether "constitutive" means essential or integral. What is beyond argument is that the synod saw the search for justice as inseparable from the preaching of the gospel.

Second, the synod acknowledged and named "structural injustice." Injustice stems not only from human sinfulness but from the way society has organized and structured its economic, social, cultural, and political life, "a network of domination, oppression, and abuses which stifle freedom."

Third, the synod did not offer easy answers, acknowledged that we cannot overcome the sin of injustice by our own efforts alone, and declared that therefore "we must *listen* with a humble and open heart to the word of God, as He shows us new paths towards action in the cause of justice in the world." The synod saw itself as an assembly where the bishops both teach and *learn.*

Fourth, the participants stressed that action on behalf of justice must begin at home, within the Church, e.g. the role of women, the lifestyle of clergy and laity.

Fifth, the synod called for effective education for justice: not simply looking to traditional values but to a fresh awakening of consciences to "a knowledge of the concrete situation," centers of social and theological research.

Strong statements, but how many Catholics are listening? Not the uncounted numbers that have heard *about* the synod's statements and still insist that the Church is waddling in politics. Somehow they have not heard that political actions often have moral implications and consequences.

In the same year as the synod, 1971, Paul VI wrote a highly important letter to Maurice Cardinal Roy, then president of the Pontifical Commission Justitia et Pax. Entitled *Octogesima adveniens* because it marked the 80th anniversary of Leo XIII's ground-breaking encyclical *Rerum novarum* (on the condition of labor), this "call to action" named a number of new social problems: urbanization, the role of youth, women's equality, the marginalized new poor, discrimination, immigration, unemployment, the media, environmental exploitation. But the letter is uncommonly significant because it reveals Paul's awareness of human experience, of the historical context, for any ecclesial reflection or action. Largely from his own extensive travels, firsthand experiences of diverse situations in which Christians found themselves, Paul could write this striking paragraph, illuminating indeed for effective *action* on behalf of justice, but also all-important for the question, To whom do we *listen?*

> In the face of such widely varying situations it is difficult for us to utter a unified message and to put forward a solution which has universal validity. Such is not our ambition, nor is it our mission. It is up to the Christian communities to analyze with objectivity the situation which is proper to their own country, to shed on it the light of the Gospel's unalterable words, and to draw principles of reflection, norms of judgment, and directives for action from the social teaching of the Church. This social teaching has been worked out in the course of history....It is up to these Christian communities, with the help of the Holy Spirit, in communion with the bishops who hold responsibility, and in dialogue with other Christian brethren and all men and women of goodwill, to discern the options and commitments which are called for in order to bring about the social, political, and economic changes seen in many cases to be urgently needed. In this search for the changes which must be promoted, Christians must first of all renew their confidence in the forcefulness and special character of the demands made by the Gospel.[25]

Note in that paragraph a process before action is taken. Not only the magisterium but the whole local community participates in the development of Catholic social teaching; not only permanent principles but analysis of the local situation; the gospel not in isolated grandeur but in dialogue with the signs of the times; the Church not only the guardian of truth which it dispenses to the world but also a pilgrim people in the world.[26]

Why is this important? Because it stresses the importance of the *community*. For all the significance of hierarchical teaching, not all the answers on social issues and action come from Rome or bishops. I find it instructive that in the last half of the 19th century and the early decades of the 20th, most of the initiatives for social reform came "from below." Indeed, Cardinal Gibbons and a small group of supporters had a positive impact on the labor movement in the United States. But "by and large the bishops of the Catholic Church did not take the initiative for social reform. The initiative came from the people and the labor movement."[27] I mean fascinating people like Terence Powderly, Irish grand master of the Knights of Labor, whose faith was shaken, and later lost, by the controversy over the Knights; labor priest Peter Dietz, organizer of the Militia of Christ for Social Service, union workers building a bridge between the Church and labor unions; Mary Kenney O'Sullivan, who began organizing shirtwaist makers and cabbies in Chicago in the 1880s; folk heroine Mother Jones, sometimes called a profane Joan of Arc, who turned on the institutional Church when it offered relief to workers in the next life alone.

In my own time, 85 years of the 20th century, lay listening and priestly hearing have complemented, at times preceded, official teaching. I am thinking of "the waterfront priest," Jesuit John M. Corridan, who heard the cries from 350 miles of New York Harbor, challenged their control by mobsters and labor racketeers, publicly condemned the hiring system on the docks, was sickened by the Communion breakfasts that paid homage to corrupt leaders, was bitterly resented by many within his own church.[28] I recall women like Dorothy Day, convert from Communism, listening to the poor by living with them, convinced that the gospel was *not* being preached to the poor. I am thinking of the amazing contributions of Catholic Charities Inc., the largest nonprofit charitable organization in the country, headed by Jesuit Fred Kammer, with 47,532 paid staff and 262,622 volunteers and board members in 1997—the vast majority lay men and women.

Listening to one another

This goes beyond listening to Jesus; this is listening to one another; this is listening in dialogue. This is listening in order to discover, discovering in order to respond. This is the parish, each parish, at its best when organizing to ask three questions:

1) What are the justice issues in our parish, in our area? Is it racial animosity? Is it immigrants threatening our precarious economic situation? Is it poverty, homelessness, our brothers and sisters sleeping on warm outdoor grates? Is it single mothers, needing a job, needing a daycare center, needing Head Start? Is it the public school, where incidentally most of our Catholic children attend? Is

it AIDS? Is it a drug culture? Is it the closing of a church or parochial school? Is it sexual abuse? Child abuse?

2) What resources—intellectual and spiritual, moral and financial—do we command to attack these issues? Many of our parishes are gifted: parishioners with money, doctors and lawyers, CEOs and CPAs, architects and real estate agents, and so into the night. Cannot they be persuaded to help? One example. In Chicago, the Jesuits have opened a school for disadvantaged Hispanic children (Cristo Rey), and businesses cooperate in hiring them a day each week, for work experience and to help with their tuition.

3) Since we cannot do everything, what shall we actually do? There is enough for the whole parish to do; there is just about no one, save for the seriously handicapped, who can not be involved in some way. Action for justice is not the private preserve of the parish or diocesan Office of Justice and Peace. A speaker in our project Preaching the Just Word has offered an analogy at once amusing and striking. Suppose, he said, that on a given Sunday, when hundreds of parishioners arrive for Mass, they are met at the church door by the Liturgy Committee en masse: "You did not have to come to Mass this morning," the chairperson announces. "We have gone to Mass for you." As a perceptive Protestant told us, "If you Catholics could get your act together, you'd be dangerous."

Men and women must listen to one another. Most of us males are heirs to a culture where decisions—in family and school, in government and church, in business and politics—were made by men. Things are a-changing, I know. Women are elected to Congress; women are CEOs in business; women sit as judges *in bamc.* Fraternities at Dartmouth College must now go coed—highly resented by alumni who recall admiringly how their own frats were the inspiration for the film *Animal House.* Within the Catholic Church, women have influential positions in our chanceries, on our tribunals. Still, radical Catholic feminists regard the Church as incorrigibly male-dominated, incapable of conversion; no conversation, therefore, in the original meaning of the Latin *conversari,* living together and talking together.

Why listen to one another? Because men and women are different in so many ways. For delight as well as insight, read two short stories by Mark Twain, "Extracts from Adam's Diary" and "Eve's Diary." Adam cannot figure Eve out. This "new creature with the long hair" is always following him about, names everything that comes along, is for ever talking, litters the whole estate with signs like "Keep Off the Grass," has a rage for explaining, says she was made out of one of his ribs, is constantly looking at herself in the pond, accuses him of being the cause of their disastrous Fall. Finally he comes to admit "I was mistaken about Eve in the beginning; it is better to live outside the Garden with her than inside without her. At first I thought she talked too much; but now I should be sorry to have that voice fall silent and pass out of my life."

To Eve, everything looks better today than it did yesterday. She thinks the other creature is a man, because it looks like one! She follows him around, curious what he might be for, finds him more interested in resting than in doing anything. He is shy, talks very little. She wishes she "could make him understand that a loving good heart is riches, and riches enough, and that without it intellect is poverty." She feels he doesn't care for anything, not even flowers, only "building shacks to coop himself up in from the good clean rain." When she unexpectedly creates fire, she wants to tell him, but no, "He would ask what it was good for, and what could I answer? for it was not *good* for something, but only beautiful, merely beautiful." She thinks she has discovered what she was made for: "to seek out the secrets of this wonderful world and be happy and thank the Giver of it all for devising it." And after the Fall? "The Garden is lost, but I have found *him,* and am content. He loves me as well as he can; I love him with all the strength of my passionate nature."

Forty years later, she prays that they may pass from this life together. "But if one of us must go first, it is my prayer that it shall be I. I am not so necessary to him as he is to me." And at Eve's grave Adam says, "Wheresoever she was, there was Eden."[29]

Yes, listening can lead to discovering, and discovering to loving.

Listening to religious voices outside

In this context, a brief but important addendum. If Catholics are not to be regrettably limited in living God's just Word, we must listen to religious voices outside our own internal Catholic experience.

First, listen to our Jewish sisters and brothers. Listen to a not inconsiderable number of Jews, fearful as they hear Americans callously claiming that the Holocaust which consumed six million of their dear ones is a gigantic hoax, never really happened. As you listen, try not to hear naked syllables. Hear voices as human as your own; hear those voices from gas chambers, from mountains of Jewish bones, teeth, hair.

Listen to Jewish leaders as they welcomed Vatican II's "Jewish Declaration" but deplored the absence therein of any note of contrition or repentance for the sufferings Jews have undergone in the Christian West. Listen to them as they quote the prince of patristic preachers, St. John Chrysostom, taking Christians of Antioch to task in 386 for thinking of Jews with respect: "The synagogue is not only a brothel and a theater; it also is a den of robbers and a lodging for wild beasts....God is not worshiped there. Heaven forbid! From now on it remains a place of idolatry."[30]

Listen to Jews as they refuse to believe with us that suffering makes for sanctity; from their experience, there is no value, spiritual or otherwise, in suffering. Suffering as redemptive? A copout, they suspect, especially coming from guilt-stricken Christians.

Listen to sympathetic Jews questioning our conviction that the message of the Prior Testament has actually been fulfilled in the New; for they can see no kingdom, no peace, no redemption. *This* is the new covenant in Christ's blood? *This* is "the day of the Lord"? *This* is a world redeemed from sin? *This* is what the Prior Testament was preparing for?

Much can be said on all those issues, but only if our response is not academic, sheerly a head trip, only if our ears are open to the Jewish experience, open to the cries from each Jewish ghetto structured by Christians, each forced baptism, each Good Friday pogrom, each forced exodus like 1492, each Dachau and each Auschwitz. Not to blame ourselves for the past, but surely to realize how wide a gulf our histories have fashioned, how much we must ponder if we are to respond justly. For to the Jew, as Elie Wiesel declared, "whoever forgets becomes the executioner's accomplice."

In February of 1999, at a critical junction in Catholic-Jewish relations, Cardinal Edward Cassidy, president of the Vatican Commission for Religious Relations with the Jews, expressed himself as concerned that some of the good work already done was being threatened. He concluded with strong counsel for all of us:

> We cannot and should not forget the past. But we must not remain chained to the past. A new and wonderful opportunity has opened up before us. Let us not miss it! *All that is required of us is to learn to listen to each other*, to seek to understand the other as the other understands him/herself, to be open to and respect the other, to work together without compromising faith or distinct identity, to be seen as children of the one and only God who know that God loves them and wants all men and women to know and experience that love, to be together a "light to the nations."[31]

Second, listen to our Protestant brothers and sisters. Here I have been fortunate; in a special way, eleven years of participation in the Lutheran-Roman Catholic Conversations. I have said it often: I was embarrassed early on, because I soon discovered that there are Protestants smarter than I am! I soon discovered what Vatican II proclaimed: Protestant churches that in the first instance are not a hindrance to the activity of God's Spirit but grace-filled communities. If that is so, then it will no longer do to say "Some of my best friends are Protestants." It is not theological enough, not ecumenical enough, not Christian enough, not Catholic enough. It behooves me to listen to them: to the graced word from many a pulpit and the graced faith in uncounted pews, to the graced life of the housewife and the graced mind of the theologian. Not necessarily to agree; there is still uncomfortably much that divides us.

Listen to them because so often these graced men and women have convictions and practices, insights and suggestions that may have escaped us. Several examples.

I have profited from the Protestant Social Gospel of the 19th century. Despite some theological inadequacy and political naïveté, many of the reforms it advocated for a just social order have been written into national legislation.

I have been instructed and inspired by the imaginative sermons of Frederick Buechner, who has suggested what the ultimate purpose of language is: so that we humans may speak to God.

I still remember and borrow Chicago theologian Joseph Sittler's insistence that the reason why we can worship nature in Vermont and manipulate nature in New York is that we have wrenched redemption from creation, have put nature "out there" and grace "in here."

For a decade I have collaborated with David H. C. Read on *The Living Pulpit*–the same Read who for three decades as minister of the Madison Avenue Presbyterian Church in New York City preached especially to what William J. Carl III called "those resident aliens and tourists who find Christianity an oddity in a nuclear age, and those expatriates and cynical citizens who have turned away from the nonsense of the gospel."

My book *Preaching the Just Word* became even more contemporary because passionate preacher/activist William Sloane Coffin persuaded me to pay specific attention, actually listen, to three urgent issues: the movement for assisted suicide, the role of women in the Catholic Church, and the rights of gays and lesbians.[32]

Chapter Four
Listen to the World

A late revered moral theologian, Redemptorist Bernard Häring, cautioned us, "If the Church doesn't listen to the world, then the world will never listen to the Church."

Pope Paul VI recognized this in an emotional address opening the second session of the Second Vatican Council on September 29, 1963. He was addressing himself to the fourth aim of the council, "The Church will build a bridge to the contemporary world." He confessed that he was tempted to be frightened and saddened, to defend and condemn, in the face of the (then) Iron Curtain, the spread of atheism, the emptiness and despair in so many human hearts; but he refused to dwell pessimistically on these aspects of human society. "Not now," he said—not while love was flooding his heart and the heart of the Church assembled in council.

Rather, Paul went on to say: "Let the world know this: the Church looks at the world with profound understanding, with sincere admiration, and with the sincere intention not of conquering it, but of serving it; not of despising it, but of appreciating it; not of condemning it, but of strengthening and saving it." He went on to address "some categories of persons with particular solicitude": the poor and needy, the suffering and sorrowing; men and women of culture and learning, scientists, artists, workers; leaders of nations; "the new generation of youth desirous of living and expressing themselves; the new peoples now coming to self-awareness, independence, and civil organization; the innumerable men and women who feel isolated in a troubled society that has no message for their spirit." To all he offered words of hope, encouragement, confidence, comfort; to all he presented the Church as a servant.[33]

How does the world speak to us? To some through firsthand experience: Dorothy Day sharing the rat-ridden quarters of the downtrodden in downtown New York; Jesuit Horace McKenna building low-cost housing for the poor in Washington, D.C. and feeding the hungry at SOME (So Others May Eat); Angelo D'Agostino, physician and Jesuit priest, off to Africa in his sixties and building treatment shelters, with private and government assistance, for little HIV-positive children.

A contemporary example closer to home: Father Michael Pfleger, pastor of St. Sabina's parish on Chicago's South Side, successfully fighting 118 billboards in his area advertising tobacco and alcohol; founding "Standing Up & Taking Notice," a social organization designed to combat crime, drugs, and abandoned property and to empower the African-American community; getting NBC to cancel Jerry Springer's violent talk show; tailed, arrested, tires slashed, bricks through his church's windows. "We have to have the heart that feels the pain and the struggle," he says. "If it doesn't make you cry anymore, then you've lost it and it's time to get out." By the way, Father Pfleger adopted two boys; a foster child he had been raising was killed in a drive-by shooting.[34]

Still, most of us hear the world through the media, from the six o'clock news to Internet. And that is important—as long as what we hear reaches the heart, does not evaporate with the last commercial. A handful of suggestions from real life.

Listening to other cultures

First, listening to the world means hearing the cries that rise to us from other cultures. One example. Granted Rome's reservations on liberation theology, I am persuaded that we might do well to take seriously Gustavo Gutiérrez's assertion with its roots in the poverty of Latin America:

> Theology is reflection, a critical attitude. Theology *follows*; it is the second step. What Hegel used to say about philosophy can likewise be applied to

theology; it rises only at sundown. The pastoral activity of the Church does not flow as a conclusion from theological premises. Theology does not produce pastoral activity; rather it reflects upon it.[35]

We may disagree, argue that this is not the only way of doing theology, but at the very least liberation theology impresses on us the need for a social analysis of actual poverty and oppression. And this demands that the ordinary intelligent Catholic, even without a higher degree, listen to what our theologians and philosophers, social scientists and historians are saying to us across our borders and waters.

Second, and in consequence, listen to the stranger. Listen the way Jesus did to the Samaritan woman (Jn 4:4–42), despised by the Jews, despising them in turn. There is no indication that he liked her; he held no brief for her lifestyle, told her frankly that her adventures in marriage were a farce, a lie. Yet he never made this a pretext for disowning her, never gave her a cold shrug of the shoulder, never said, "Forget the drink, lady; your hands are unclean." He not only spoke to her; he listened to her. Because of that fascinating conversation, she turned from sinner to apostle, rushed back to the people in her town, asked them, "He cannot be the Messiah, can he?" (v. 29). And crowds came out to see this surprising stranger, had him stay with them for two days, asserted that their new-found faith was no longer dependent on her story; they had heard it from the mouth of this stranger.

In our time a special kind of stranger is the immigrant, the legal as well as the illegal: a stranger to our prevailing culture, a stranger all too often in our Catholic churches. Here the Christian virtue of hospitality is more than coffee and doughnuts, more than an occasional Mariachi Mass. It's listening. Hear their story. Not in self-defense, aware that in half a century they will outnumber Catholic palefaces. Rather because they are our sisters and brothers in Christ before they are potential subverters of our economy. Traveling across the country, I am learning how difficult it is to integrate a large number of Hispanics or Vietnamese or Filipinos into a totally Caucasian community; the cultures are so different, the languages a barrier. Still, I believe, a beginning of welcome is not only a broad smile but an open ear. Remember: To listen means to discover, and discovering will demand a response.

Listening to African-Americans

Third, listen to our African-American sisters and brothers. They still cry to us, as the Lord cried to Pharaoh, "Let my people go" (Exod 5:1). A disproportionate number of black people are poor. As Sister Thea Bowman told the U.S. bishops, "Poverty, deprivation, stunted physical, intellectual and spiritual growth—more than a third of the black people that live in the United States live in poverty, the kind of poverty that lacks basic necessity....A disproportionate number of our men are dying of suicide and AIDS and drug abuse and low self-esteem."[36]

What do I hear? Naked statistics? Or persons, each an image of God? Listening that demands a response, at times a change of attitude. Racism is not dead in our land; it has gone undercover. Like the priest in Jesus' story, do I "pass by on the other side" (Lk 10:31)?

A troubling reality: Hate has a new face clean-cut, a new voice softer-spoken, has learned how to sell itself more effectively. "White supremacists" are now antigovernment "patriots." Klan cross burnings yield to "sacred cross lightings." As of 1998, 254 hate sites operated on the Internet. A racist lawyer, refused admittance to Illinois's state bar because of his white-supremacist views, flaunted his victimhood on TV for weeks. Notes a member of Klanwatch, a project of the Southern Poverty Law Center: "Instead of saying, 'The dirty Mexicans are stealing our jobs,' they say, 'We are overwhelmed by immigration.'" Good advice for listeners: "Monitor the racists, but don't make them martyrs."[37]

Listening to land mines

Fourth, listen to another ceaseless cry from the world, this one movingly muted: "Every 22 minutes a woman, man, or child somewhere in the world is maimed or killed outright by a land mine. Scattered throughout dozens of countries—most of them among the poorest—an estimated 70 million of these lethal devices lie in wait."[38] Many are listening and protesting: Physicians against Landmines; UNICEF; Senator Patrick J. Leahy of Vermont; 15 retired generals, including Norman Schwartzkopf; the U.S. bishops; John Paul II. On March 1, 1999, the Ottawa Mine Ban Treaty (Convention on the Prohibition, Use, Stockpiling, Production and Transfer of Anti-Personnel Mines and on Their Destruction) went into effect, signed as of that date by 134 countries, ratified by 65 of them. But not by Russia and China, Iran and Iraq, and many more. Not by the United States, which will not end its use of mines till 2003, and even then not in Korea, unless suitable alternatives are found. As I write, new reports tell me that not only is the United States not signing the Ottawa Treaty, but the Clinton Administration is seeking from Congress $48.3 million to be spent on a new type of artillery-fired land-mine system designed to destroy tanks and people. In that context Senator Leahy is planning to introduce new legislation that would move the United States closer to treaty compliance even if it does not sign the treaty.

In that mélange, where do you stand? Have you heard the cries of land-mine victims? In fairness to the U.S. position, how do you balance the ceaseless destruction, the fact that "for every mine removed, as many as 10 more are sown,"[39] with the danger to our troops in Korea if the mines there are removed and no alternatives exist?

Listening to cries for forgiveness

"America," an Easter issue of *Time* magazine asserted, "can be a very unforgiving place."[40] Strange. On Easter Sunday millions of Christians celebrate the very incarnation of forgiveness, the risen Lord. Apart from forgiveness Bethlehem and Calvary make no sense. We listen not only to Jesus' first words from Calvary, "Father, forgive them" (Lk 23:34). We listen to a crib and a cross that are themselves mute cries, unforgettable cries, for forgiveness. The cross echoes Jesus' parables of forgiveness: the prodigal son, the good shepherd. The cross recalls Jesus' strong warning, "If you do not forgive others, neither will your Father forgive your trespasses" (Mt 6:15).

The problem is not with Jesus. Nor can we ourselves be accused of not listening, because

> ...the problem with forgiveness has been that of all acknowledged good acts, it is the one we are most suspicious of. "To err is human, to forgive, supine," punned S. J. Perelman. In a country where the death penalty has been a proven vote getter in recent years, forgiveness is often seen as effete and irresponsible. Sometimes it even seems to condone the offense, as noted centuries ago by Jewish sages who declared, "He that is merciful to the cruel will eventually be cruel to the innocent."[41]

Happily, forgiveness is far from dead. One example. In 1992, 16-year-old Amy Fisher knocked on the door of Mary Jo Buttafuoco in Massapequa, Long Island, and shot her in the head. At the time she was having sex with Mary Jo's husband. Through letters not long ago, Amy won Mary Jo's forgiveness. They met in court and brushed fingers. "Through faith in God," Mary Jo admitted, "I am able to forgive. It did not come easily or quickly."[42] Mary Jo listened, not only to Amy but to God.

Listening to nonhuman creation

Fifth, listen to God's nonhuman creation. How many of us have heard John Paul II declare that Christians must "realize that their responsibility within creation and their duty toward nature and the Creator are *an essential part of their faith*"?[43] How many believe it? How many live it?

What response, in concrete living, does listening to John Paul on creation and nature involve? For one thing, an end to consumerism. The pope told us what he had in mind: "an excessive availability of every kind of material goods for the benefit of certain social groups, [which] easily makes people slaves of 'possession' and of immediate gratification, with no other horizon than the multiplication or continual replacement of the things already owned with others still better."[44] This itself goes back to a basic principle of Christian humanism, stressed by Vatican II in the wake of Pope Paul VI: being over having. Men and women are more precious for what they are than for what they possess.[45] It is not a clear conviction in our culture. Sports, entertainment, business, communication—the sign of our times is the dollar sign.

There is little reason to believe that most Christians are significantly different from their non-Christian neighbors where consumerism is concerned.

No less an apostle than St. Paul was inspired to tell us that God's material "creation has been groaning in labor pains until now," has been "waiting with eager longing" to be "set free from its bondage to decay," to "obtain the freedom of the glory of the children of God" (Rom 8:19–22). As Paul saw it, ever since Adam's sin nonhuman creation has existed in an abnormal state, a state of frustration, subject to corruption and decay. Strange as it may sound to us, difficult as it is to explain it adequately, Paul was affirming a solidarity of the human and subhuman world in the redemption of Christ. "Material creation," biblical expert Joseph Fitzmyer claims, "is thus not to be a mere spectator of humanity's triumphant glory and freedom, but to share in it. When the children of God are finally revealed in glory, the material world will also be emancipated from the 'last enemy.'"[46]

A complex theology, indeed; but Francis of Assisi lived it, and John Paul II is convinced of it.

Listening to America's children

Sixth, and perhaps most agonizing of all, listen to our children. Yes, *our* children. In 1973, 14.4 percent of all children in the United States were poor; by 1996 the rate had grown to 20.5 percent. For young families the rate doubled: from 20 percent in 1973 to 41 percent in 1994.[47] In our fair land, the younger you are the poorer you are. In 1996, 40.3 percent of Hispanic children, 39.9 percent of black children, and 16.3 percent of white children were poor.[48] About 3.1 million children have been reported abused and/or neglected. In 1996 an estimated 502,000 children were in foster care on an average day. In 1997 between 3.5 million and 4 million children ages 9–17 had serious emotional disturbance.[49] In my own back yard, the District of Columbia, children have been preparing their own funerals: how they want to look, how to be dressed, where to be waked. They simply do not believe they will be around very long; in one five-year period 224 of their childhood friends died from gunfire. And listen to children's expert Sylvia Hewlett: In the United States there are greater tax benefits for breeding horses than for producing children.

These are not naked statistics. Poverty steals children's potential. Iron deficiency causes anemia, impairs problem solving, motor coordination, attention, and concentration. Hunger induces fatigue, dizziness, irritability, headaches, ear infections, weight loss, frequent colds. Stunted growth makes for learning problems.[50]

Do we hear the children crying?

Chapter Five

What Listening Involves

A bit of clarification. I am not implying that listening will remove all doubts, all difficulties; that responding will be automatically triggered by listening; that the response will be identical among all who respond. Here are some practical suggestions.

Four practical precepts

It may sound strange at first hearing, but a high-powered Jesuit theologian, the late Bernard Lonergan, has provided what is at once a genuinely theological and a splendidly practical program for listening. He calls his four precepts "transcendental," because they underlie all our categories and are ways in which we transcend ourselves.[51]

The precepts: Be attentive, be intelligent, be reasonable, be responsible. The precepts actually spell out what we have seen as listen, discover, and respond. Let me apply these to concrete issues of justice.

First, be *attentive*. Jesus insisted on that to his disciples and others who had gathered around: "Pay attention to what you hear" (Mk 4:24). Lonergan meant: Give full rein to your experience. Know the data, the facts.

One example. On the wall of my office in Northwest Washington, D.C., I have taped a photograph, a picture that meets my eyes each time I enter, often when I leave. It shows a young boy, perhaps ten years old, a little over five feet high. He is standing in the middle of a gigantic garbage dump somewhere in Brazil. His cap, on backwards, half covers a mop of filthy hair. His face is almost hidden behind dirt and soot; his eyes stare at me unblinking; his mouth is closed tight, the ends of his lips down, sullen. His hands are stuffed into the pockets of pants that will never be clean again. His shoes are all but planted in mud. This is where he works. He is a scavenger. He collects used paper, plastics, rags, and bottles from garbage dumps and sells them to retailers for recycling. Among the most hazardous of jobs, destructive of health as well as of hope. I grace my wall with this photo because it compels me to listen, forces me to hear the children crying, children who have no lobby comparable to the tobacco industry's. Here is raw data on child labor.

But the raw data are not enough. Second, be *intelligent*. What's going on here? And why? The ten-year-old in my photo is an image of the unimaginable abuse children still endure across the world as we celebrate the end of a century that for violence may have no parallel in history.

To be *intelligent,* I must rid myself of four myths about child labor.[52] Myth 1: Child labor only happens in the poor world. Fact: Untrue; even in our United States "children are exploited in garment industry sweatshops."[53] Myth 2: Child labor will never be eliminated until poverty disappears, and poverty will always be with us. Fact: "Children would not be harmed by work if there were not people prepared and able to exploit them. And child labor, in fact, can actually perpetuate poverty...."[54] Myth 3: Child labor occurs primarily in export industries. Fact: Probably less than five percent of all child workers are employed in export-sector industries. Myth 4: The only way to make headway against child labor is for consumers and governments to apply pressure through sanctions and boycotts. Fact: Activists and organizations, local and international, have been working in developing countries for years on issues of child abuse. Sanctions affect only export industries. "And sanctions are also blunt instruments with long-term consequences that may not be foreseen, with the result that they harm, instead of help, children."[55]

Third, be *reasonable:* Marshal the evidence, examine the opinions, judge with wisdom. Not easy to do, especially when you are not an expert in a field. Hence the need for community cooperation; the Lone Ranger is an endangered species.

In Latin America, parents are often unemployed and their children are offered the jobs. Why? Because children can be paid less; children will do what they are told;

children are less likely to organize; children can be physically abused without striking back. In a word, children are easier to exploit.

But listen to the employers. Many claim they have to pay less to survive. Others unashamedly see exploitation of children as a natural part of the existing social order. Some in India insist that low-caste children should work rather than go to school; otherwise fields will be left uncultivated.[56] Judge with wisdom.

Fourth, be *responsible:* Do something about it. Act on the basis of prudent judgments and genuine values. Here fear can limit what we hear. The fearful question is: What am *I* to do about it? The fear is not unreasonable. For one thing, sheer time waves its inexorable hand in your face; you have other responsibilities—your job, your family, your education. You cannot leave home for India or Indonesia; but cannot you, cannot the parish, do something about poverty in your area? Can you keep one youngster from dropping out of high school because he has to support an ailing mother? Does it sound dreadfully minimal? Not if you are one of several hundred thousand similarly responsible.

Need for a spirituality

Not a simple task this listening, not if you are willing to be attentive, intelligent, reasonable, and responsible. From this I conclude that genuine listening is more likely to happen if you are gifted with a real relationship to God. For a Christian, the response to injustice is not a work of unaided human intelligence, high energy, personal initiative, strong will, masterly productivity. Pertinent here are the strong words of Jesus in his last discourse (Jn 15:4-5):

> Remain in me as I remain in you.
> Just as a branch cannot bear fruit by itself
> without remaining on the vine,
> so neither can you bear fruit without remaining in
>   me.
> I am the vine, you are the branches.
> He who remains in me and I in him
> is the one who bears much fruit,
> for apart from me you can do nothing.

Apart from Jesus, separated from Jesus, you and I "can do nothing." Oh yes, apart from Jesus we can eat and sleep, work and play, make a million and raise a family, speak a kind word here and do a charitable work there. But, in a genuinely Catholic theology, it is only with the favor of God we call "grace" that we can do anything that moves us positively in the direction of salvation. And such, I submit, are our efforts to live biblical justice: fidelity to God, to people, to the earth. Our hopes for effective involvement are based in St. Paul's simple admission to the Christians at Philippi in Macedonia, "I can do all things through [the Lord] who strengthens me" (Phil 4:13). Through the Lord.

In this area the late Cardinal Joseph Bernardin of Chicago has been instructive to me. His decade as archbishop of Cincinnati he called "the greatest blessing in my priesthood." Of this he wrote:

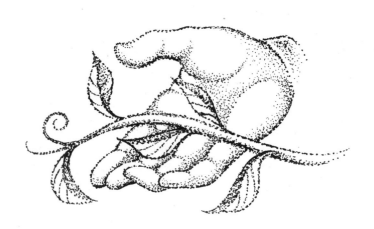

The priests of Cincinnati were especially helpful for my spiritual growth. Several years ago I sensed that administrative responsibilities were eating away at my interior life. I told several young priests that I felt they were praying more and better than I. I told them I wanted and needed their help. They generously took me into their lives of prayer and helped me come closer to the Lord. Theirs was a wonderful and permanent gift.[57]

His priest friend John Hotchkin recalls that "After this Cincinnati prayer experience, the skilled and gifted ecclesiastical administrator became someone indefinably different, a person of hope, not just a person of plans and expectations, but a true person of hope, hope that because it clings to the person of Jesus cannot be derailed."[58] Bernardin listened. Without explicitly using Lonergan's transcendental precepts, he gathered the data on his interior life, analyzed the data, studied the pros and cons, and came to a major decision: He had to change his life. The administrator still administered, the archbishop still supervised, but as a man of profound prayer. Not separated from administration; enriching it—and himself.

How do men and women of biblical justice get that way? In close union with Christ our Lord. How shall we change our world, its rugged individualism, its excessive consumerism, its growing violence, its deep-rooted racism? *We* shall not; *God* will do it, or it will not happen. And still, God will normally do it *through us*. Through men and women whose dynamism for change is not their own naked humanity but the power of God. God needs us, but only because God wants to need us, wants humanity to cooperate with divinity in the love that saves a world. But remember, even our cooperation is grace, is a gift. Listen to Paul again, this time to the Christians of Corinth (1 Cor 1:26–31):

> Consider your own call, brothers and sisters. Not many of you were wise by human standards, not many were powerful, not many were of noble birth. But God chose what is foolish in the world to shame the wise; God chose what is weak in the world to shame the strong; God chose what is insignificant and despised in the world, things that are not, to reduce to nothing things that are, so that no one might boast in the presence of God. He is the source of your life in Christ Jesus, who became our wisdom from God, our justification, our sanctification, and our redemption.

This calls not only for an occasional prayer but for a conversion, perhaps a sea change; it demands a spirituality, specifically of justice. It means that, baptized into Christ, we relate to God, to people, and to the earth not as rugged individualists but as part and parcel of a people, members of a body where, as St. Paul insisted, no one can say to any other, "I have no need of you" (1 Cor 12:21). By God's gracious giving, we are commissioned by Christ to be channels of grace to one another. The justice aspect of this reality has been put briefly and pungently by theologian Jon Sobrino:

"When the Church has taken the poor seriously, it is then that it has become truly apostolic. When the Church goes out to them in mission, the paradoxical result is that they, the poor, evangelize the Church."[59] Biblical justice is not a one-way street. The poor, the disadvantaged, the downtrodden are not just recipients of justice ministry; they are our teachers and educators—if we have ears to hear.

This community facet of justice (remember, fidelity to relationships) should find its highest expression and richest source in the Eucharist. Why? Vatican II stated our Catholic tradition with admirable succinctness: "The liturgy is the summit to which the Church's activity is directed; at the same time it is the source from which all her power proceeds....From the liturgy, therefore, and especially from the Eucharist,...that sanctification of men and women in Christ and the glorification of God, to which all other activities of the Church stretch and strain as toward their goal, are most effectively achieved."[60]

How can this be? Not because the Eucharist supplies concrete answers to specific issues. Rather because good liturgy, liturgy loved and lived, can be a powerful force for conversion, for liberation. For it can make us aware of our addictions and illusions, can free us from a confining concentration on ourselves, can loose us from an ice-cold isolation. Positively, good liturgy can open our ears to the other: to God, to people, to the earth. Good liturgy can restore relationships. Not by a simple handclasp after the communal Our Father; rather by a participation in the Eucharist that is no longer routine and habit but a conscious communion with *this* congregation, with the

Church around the world, and with the unnumbered holy men and women who have gone before us as a community of the redeemed. Relationships? Nothing on earth can compare with it.

Danger of a closed heart

Here I suggest a bit of meditation material shaped by imaginative Jesuit William J. O'Malley from Matthew 13:14-17:

> "The reason I teach you in stories," Jesus said,
> "is that your eyes are open but sightless, dead.
> Your ears prick up and hear only silence.
> You listen and listen, and understand nothing;
> you peer about, and peer, but never perceive.
> For your heart is tough as a tightened fist,
> your ears echo like empty shells,
> your eyes clamp shut for fear of what you will see.
> Open! Hear! See! Me."[61]

The problem? At times we hear without understanding because so often our hearts are closed. Not deliberately; at times we are not even aware of a heart "tough as a tightened fist." But there we can easily be. And not necessarily or exclusively as we grow older and tend to restrict our relationships, as we find others' problems less bearable burdens. Young hearts, for all their resiliency, can be quite narrow.

Some examples of closed hearts I have myself experienced across the country on justice issues: "No one will ever persuade me that people on welfare are not lazy; anybody can get a job if he really wants to." "You kill somebody, you die, that's justice, that's what you deserve, and anybody but a fool can see that capital punishment cuts down crime." "Immigrants are stealing our jobs because they're willing to work for less." "AIDS is God's punishment on the promiscuous." And so on deep into the night. Only God's grace can break through hardened hearts. Perhaps an urgent prayer from the heart will help: "In my own Gethsemane, Jesus, help me to say as you said to the Father, 'Not what I want, but only what you want.'" More surely, a rounded spirituality rooted in a faithful Christian community and in an all-powerful Eucharist.

Too much to do and too little time?

I am keenly aware of a nagging problem here: Listening to the injustices that plague the world can lead to despondency, hopelessness, almost despair. The issues are overwhelming and I am so powerless. I listen to the cries from Rwanda: orchestrated genocide that butchered a million out of eight million people. I listen to the cries of children in Northern Ireland, their blood begging for the tremulous peace that threatens to dissolve tomorrow. I listen to cries from the Middle East, from Palestinians and Israelis alike, and I wonder how age-old enmities can ever be resolved. Even here at home I listen to little ones hungry, abused, orphaned, homeless; to youngsters gunned down by their schoolmates; to African-Americans still suffering from a now latent racism; to Native Americans homeless in their own homeland, afflicted by joblessness, alcoholism, and our indifference; to the pope decrying a culture of consumerism, a culture of death. What can one person, or a small community, do?

A practical principle: Think globally, act locally. Choose an area of injustice that is actual, that touched you when you listened to it, that seems doable, that already involves others.

One example. Not long ago, the Catholic Committee of Appalachia launched a campaign in solidarity with those homes and ways of life being impoverished by an invasive mining practice and in affirmation of a Christian community that respects creation. How bring their day-to-day decisions and actions in line with their moral principles? The campaign, "Powering Down: A Less Is More Proposal," encouraged the faithful to make the first Friday of each month a day of sacrifice and self-denial. Specifically, abstain as much as possible from the use of electricity and fossil fuels. Concrete acts of solidarity? Reduce heating and air conditioning; turn off TV or radio; eat a cold meal or share a single-pot meal with others; use public transportation or car-pooling; arrange office work to reduce computer use; make and use a solar cooker. All this to be embraced as a day of Jubilee (Leviticus 25), to allow their lives some fallow time: time to be with family and friends, reconnect with the natural rhythms of sunrise and sunset, leave space for actions that embody justice and respect.[62]

Small, yes. But from small beginnings.... Remember "O little town of Bethlehem"?

Your parish probably has, your diocese surely has, an Office of Justice and Peace. Join up. See to it that it has intimate links to the Office of Education. All too rarely do they come together.

Allow me to end on a highly hopeful note. God is wherever you and I are. It can, of course, be a frightening thought if I am fleeing from God; on the other hand, it is a shot of adrenalin if I am looking for God. But I have to listen to God, I have to let...God...talk.

We have seen that the Lord can talk to us in ever so many ways. Not only through the word that is Scripture, not only through church teaching, but also through voices outside our own ecclesiastical life, voices that express the joys and sorrows, the hope and anguish of a world. The Lord can talk to us through Beethoven and the Beatles, through nuclear threat and chemical waste, through AIDS victims and ladies of the night, through friends whose caring reflects the compassion of Christ and ayatollahs who identify America with Satan, through wealth and poverty, power and helplessness, fame and humiliation. But our ears must be open, attuned to God's whisper as well as to God's thunder. Like the boy Samuel in the Prior Testament, I have to say "Speak, Lord, for your servant is listening" (1 Sam 3:9). Not, as Princeton ethicist Paul Ramsey perceptively put it, "Speak, Lord, and your servant will think it over." Not that listening precludes thinking; only, once it is clear that it is God speaking, a response cannot be avoided.

One way of simplifying all this: Listen to your life. To do that well, you must recall time and again that human living, your living and mine, is a matter of relationships: to God, to people, to the earth. It is, in its small way, a share in the life of the Trinity; for the Trinity is defined by relationships: The Father gives Being to the Son from all eternity; the Son responds to the Father in love eternal; the love of Father and Son *is* a person, the Holy Spirit. Here is the model without beginning for every love that has ever begun: I-and-Thou indeed, distinct persons, but never mine-and-thine, those ice-cold words. The model, without beginning or end, for our own lives of justice.

Listen, then, to the way you live each day, each relationship; monitor the way life in relationship passes by. "See [your life] for the fathomless mystery that it is. In the boredom and pain of it no less than in the excitement and gladness: touch, taste, smell your way to the holy and hidden heart of it because in the last analysis all moments are key moments, and life itself is grace."[63]

A pertinent item has just come my way, a quotation whose source is unknown: "Leadership according to the World: We lead more by what we say than by listening. Leadership according to the Gospel: We lead more by listening than by what we say."

Amen.

Notes

1. C. F. D. Moule, *The Gospel according to Mark* (London: Cambridge University Press, 1965) 38.

2. Quoted in Paul Wilkes, "The Education of an Archbishop," *New Yorker*, July 15, 1991, 38–59, at 44.

3. Frederick Buechner, *Now and Then* (San Francisco: Harper & Row, 1983) 3.

4. For more detailed information, see my *Preaching the Just Word* (New Haven: Yale University Press, 1996).

5. Philip Land, S.J., "Justice," *The New Dictionary of Theology*, ed. Joseph A. Komonchak, Mary Collins, and Dermot A. Lane (Wilmington, Del.: Michael Glazier, 1987) 548–53, at 548–49.

6. John R. Donahue, S.J., "Biblical Perspectives on Justice," in *The Faith That Does Justice: Examining the Christian Sources for Social Change*, ed. John C. Haughey, S.J. (Woodstock Studies 1; New York: Paulist Press, 1977) 68–112, at 69; italics in text.

7. Daniel J. Harrington, S.J., *The Gospel of Matthew* (Sacra pagina 1; Collegeville, Minn.: Liturgical Press, 1991) 66.

8. Paul VI, *Evangelization in the Modern World,* nos. 29 and 36 (tr. *The Pope Speaks* 21, no. 1 [spring 1976] 17 and 20).

9. Message for the World Day of Peace, "Peace with God the Creator, Peace with All of Creation," Jan. 1, 1990; English text, "Peace with All Creation," *Origins* 19, no. 28 (Dec. 14, 1989) 465–68; quotation from no. 15, p. 468; emphasis mine.

10. Fergus Kerr, O.P., "Theology in a Godforsaken Epoch," *Blackfriars* 46 (1965) 665–72, at 665.

11. Constitution on the Sacred Liturgy, no. 7.

12. See Joseph A. Fitzmyer, *The Gospel according to Luke (I–IX)* (Garden City, N.Y.: Doubleday, 1981) 533–34.

13. *St. Athanasius: The Life of St. Antony* 2, tr. Robert T. Meyer (Ancient Christian Writers 10; New York, N.Y./Ramsey, N.J.: Newman, 1950/1978) 19.

14. From George Weigel, "The Pope, the President, and the Rest of Us," *Catholic Standard* (Washington, D.C.) 49, no. 9 (Feb. 18, 1999) 12.

15. *Washington Post,* Jan. 5, 1997, C7.

16. From Patricia Lefevere, "Hail to the Chiefs," (London) *Tablet,* Feb. 6, 1999, 192–94, at 193. Lefevere, a religion writer based in New York City, was commenting on Pope John Paul's January 1999 visit to St. Louis; the title refers to the meeting there between pope and president.

17. Robert M. Morgenthau, Op-Ed, "What Prosecutors Won't Tell You," *New York Times,* Feb. 7, 1995.

18. Letters to the Editor, *Washington Post*, May 19, 1998, A20.

19. John Paul II, encyclical *The Gospel of Life* 56 (tr. *Origins* 24, n. 42 [April 6, 1995] 709).

20. George M. Anderson, S.J., "Fourteen Years on Death Row: An Interview with Joseph Green Brown," *America*, March 29, 1997, 17–20, at 18.

21. Quotations are taken from Kenneth J. Fanelli, "Advocating Forgiveness," *CUA Magazine* [Catholic University of America] 11, no. 1 (winter 1999) 10–11.

22. Vatican II, Dogmatic Constitution on Divine Revelation, no. 8 (tr. *The Documents of Vatican II*, ed. Walter M. Abbott, S.J. [New York: Herder and Herder, 1966] 116).

23. *De iustitia in mundo* (Vatican Press, 1971).

24. My summary owes much to Marvin L. Hrier Mich, *Catholic Social Teaching and Movements* (Mystic, Conn.: Twenty-third, 1998) 192–95.

25. Paul VI, *Octogesima adveniens*, no. 4. I am using the official English translation as reproduced by Mary Elsbernd, O.S.F., "What Ever Happened to *Octogesima adveniens?*" *Theological Studies* 56 (1995) 39–60, at 42. I have presumed to add "and women" to "all men," to capture more discreetly the full meaning of the Latin *homines* in our day.

26. See Elsbernd, ibid. 59–60. She is convinced that recent Catholic social teaching, as in John Paul II, is not characterized by participation, and that this downplays the power of social, political, religious, and economic structures and movements to shape lives and meaning.

27. Hrier Mich, *Catholic Social Teaching and Movements* 47.

28. For details see James T. Fisher, "John M. Corridan, S.J., and the Battle for the Soul of the Waterfront, 1948–1954," *U.S. Catholic Historian* 16, no. 4 (fall 1998) 71–87.

29. From *The Signet Classic Book of Mark Twain's Short Stories*, ed. Justin Kaplan (Markham, Ont.: New American Library [Penguin Books], 1985) 317–39.

30. *Discourse 1 against Judaizing Christians* 3.1–3.

31. Text under title "Uncertain Atmosphere Clouds Catholic-Jewish Relations," *Origins* 28, no. 37 (March 4, 1999) 641, 643–45, at 645.

32. For an account of the listening and the struggling, see *Preaching the Just Word* (n. 4 above) 84–120.

33. Translations from Michael Novak, *The Open Church: Vatican II, Act II* (New York: Macmillan, 1964) 84–87.

34. See Tim Unsworth, "Pfleger Faces Down the Philistines," *U.S. Catholic*, March 1999, 22–25.

35. Gustavo Gutiérrez, *A Theology of Liberation* (Maryknoll, N.Y.: Orbis, 1973) 11.

36. I am borrowing from the text in *Sister Thea Bowman, Shooting Star: Selected Writings and Speeches*, ed. Celestine Cepress, FSPA (Winona, Minn.: Saint Mary's Press, 1993) 31.

37. See John Cloud, "Trading White Sheets for Pinstripes," *Time* 153, no. 9 (March 8, 1999) 30–31.

38. Editorial, "Land Mines: Another Pro-Life Issue," *America* 180, no. 6 (Feb. 27, 1999) 3.

39. Ibid.

40. David Van Biema, "Should All Be Forgiven?" *Time* 153, no. 13 (April 5, 1999) 54–58, at 55.

41. Ibid.

42. *USA Today,* April 23, 1999, 6A.

43. John Paul II, "Peace with All Creation," *Origins* 19, no. 28 (Dec. 14, 1989) 465–68; quotation from no. 8; emphasis mine.

44. John Paul II, encyclical letter *On Social Concern* (Dec. 30, 1987) no. 28 (tr. United States Catholic Conference, Washington, D.C., Publication No. 205-5, pp. 48–49); emphasis in text.

45. See Vatican II, Pastoral Constitution on the Church in the Modern World, no. 35; Paul VI, Address to the Diplomatic Corps, Jan. 7, 1965 (*Acta apostolicae sedis* 57 [1965] 232).

46. Joseph A. Fitzmyer, S.J., "The Letter to the Romans," *The New Jerome Biblical Commentary,* ed. Raymond E. Brown, S.S., Joseph A. Fitzmyer, S.J., and Roland E. Murphy, O.Carm. (Englewood Cliffs, N.J.: Prentice-Hall, 1990) 51:87, p. 854.

47. Statistics from the Census Bureau, as reported in the Children's Defense Fund's *The State of America's Children: Yearbook 1998* (Washington, D.C.: Children's Defense Fund, 1998) 3.

48. Ibid., 4.

49. Ibid., 66.

50. For more details see Arloc Sherman, *Wasting America's Future: The Children's Defense Fund Report on the Cost of Child Poverty* (Boston: Beacon, 1994) xv, xviii–xix.

51. See Bernard J. F. Lonergan, S.J., *Method in Theology* (New York: Herder and Herder, 1972) esp. 14–15, 55, 238–42, 357, 363.

52. I take these from Carol Bellamy, *The State of the World's Children 1997* (New York: Oxford University Press, 1997) 18–24. The photo appears on page 16.

53. Ibid., 17.

54. Ibid., 20.

55. Ibid., 23.

56. See ibid., 27.

57. Joseph Bernardin, *It Is Christ We Preach* (Boston: St. Paul Editions, 1982) 13.

58. John Hotchkin, "Cardinal Bernardin: A True Person of Hope," *Origins* 26, no. 25 (Dec. 5, 1966) 409–11, at 410–11.

59. Quoted by John F. Talbot, S.J., "Who Evangelizes Whom? The Poor Evangelizers," *Review for Religious,* November-December 1993, 896, from Sobrino's *Resurrección de la verdadera Iglesia* 137–38.

60. Constitution on the Sacred Liturgy, no. 10.

61. William J. O'Malley, S.J., *Daily Prayers for Busy People* (Winona, Minn.: Saint Mary's Press, 1990) 180.

62. Details from Carol E. Warren, "Power Down in Solidarity with All Creation," *National Catholic Reporter* 35, no. 15 (Feb. 12, 1999) 22. The author was writing from Webster Springs, W.Va.

63. Buechner, *Now and Then* (n. 3 above) 87.

ILLUMINATIONBOOKS

Other Books in the Series

Love God...Clean House...Help Others
        by Duane F. Reinert, O.F.M. Cap.

Along Your Desert Journey
        by Robert M. Hamma

Appreciating God's Creation Through Scripture
        by Alice L. Laffey

Let Yourself Be Loved
        by Phillip Bennett

Facing Discouragement
        by Kathleen Fischer and Thomas Hart

Living Simply in an Anxious World
        by Robert J. Wicks

A Rainy Afternoon with God
        by Catherine B. Cawley

Time, A Collection of Fragile Moments
        by Joan Monahan

15 Ways to Nourish Your Faith
        by Susan Shannon Davies

Following in the Footsteps of Jesus
        by Gerald D. Coleman, S.S. and David M. Pettingill

God Lives Next Door
        by Lyle K. Weiss